Blockchain: The comprehensive beginner's guide to learn Blockchain with its innovative technology and Modern Financial Framework that will improve and revolutionize the Next Digital Economy

----- ❧ -----

FRANK WALRTIN

The trademarks that are used are without any consent, and the publication of the trademark is without permission or backing by the trademark owner. All trademarks and brands within this book are for clarifying purposes only and are the owned by the owners themselves, not affiliated with this document.

The material on this book is for informational purposes only. As each individual situation is unique, you should use proper discretion, in consultation with a health care practitioner, before undertaking the protocols, diet, exercises, techniques, training methods, or otherwise described herein. The author and publisher expressly disclaim responsibility for any adverse effects that may result from the use or application of the information contained herein.

Table of Contents

Introduction

Thank you for downloading this book!

You have probably picked up this book because you have learned about the current hype about blockchains, but chances are, you do not even know what they are and why they actually matter. This book is designed to answer most, if not all, of the questions that you have about this technology in a manner that truly speaks to you.

Blockchain is changing the way people view trust and security in their daily life – imagine a world wherein data is truly secured, centralized, and free from the risk of misinterpretation. While this may seem to be a farfetched idea, this technology is already being eased in into every business that is part of your life.

While blockchain may seem like a jargon right now, most of the things that you encounter in your daily life is bound to be changed by this concept. This seemingly future concept is already here and is slowly being adapted in economics, trade, and even in the simplest transactions that you do.

It is predicted that in two decades, blockchains will change the world the way internet did forty years ago. Are you ready for the future?

Chapter 1:

What is Blockchain?

Since the time of clay tablets, people have recorded exchanges of goods and services. As the digital age changed the way human beings transact with others, methods of recording these exchanges has evolved and has become increasingly complex. Nowadays, people do not just need to monitor a single exchange – they need to know how supplies are delivered, if money exchanged over the internet is received, how products are manufactured and packaged, and so on. The growth of trade, or even the way people communicate with each other, created a need for people to rely on large databases that carry great amounts of ledgers.

Since 2016, a lot of talk has been given about blockchain, a revolutionary technology that is thought to change the way people think about currency, exchanges, and even the way people store and send data. This means that this technology is set to change the way people transact with each other. However, while blockchain is widely-thought to change the future, not many people know what it is really about.

While blockchain may seem to be a jargon right now, it is believed to have wide-reaching implications that will change many, if not all, industries and businesses all over the world.

The Issue of Trust

If there is one thing that blockchain majorly changes, it is the concept of trust. You are likely to only deal with businesses that you are sure you can depend on, in exchange for your hard-earned money. At the same time, you will definitely not want to deal with anyone that has a bad reputation.

However, most people experience a trust gap whenever they transact with someone – it is simply too easy for anyone to create a Facebook page or a website that would make them appear trustworthy to others. When it comes to public records, you may also have the idea that you can never be sure if a record is tampered in the past. It is always easy to remove or replace a record in order to swindle someone his money. Because people are experiencing a trust gap on most transactions that they do online, most people are forced to go back to offline modes of transacting, which can be tedious, time-consuming, expensive, and is also likely to experience errors.

This is also the reason why people have trusted institutions, such as banks, monitoring committees, credit investigators, and so on, in place. People need to have intermediaries or third party institutions in order to make sure that their interests are protected and that they will not be victimized when they transact with others. People need a safe place to store their data, as well as credible sources of information when they do business, and to date, people are paying for the cost of these intermediaries' services.

However, if people can find a way to develop trust while using the internet and commit to doing online transactions without fear of fraud or data manipulation, then you get the idea that exchanges will be done faster and more securely.

Defining Blockchain

Blockchain is a decentralized ledger of transactions. You can think of blockchain as a big database of records that is managed by different people, including you – instead of relying on certain institutions to manage your data. You can think of it as a spreadsheet that is sent over a network of computers, which is created in order to regulate the spreadsheet so everyone can make sure every record in it is correct.

Just like what the term blockchain implies, each step of every transaction is stored as a block, which connects to everything that comes after it. These blocks are stored in a network, wherein everybody has a copy of the block, so they can be easily pulled up. However, each block is protected by a key so it doesn't get tampered with by the people within the network.

What does that mean, then? Right now, every paperwork or record that matters to you is handled by an institution that you trust – banks, the government, insurance providers, credit card companies, human resources, and other similar bodies exist because of the principle of trust that people provide them. Because they operate with the virtue of trust, these institutions are the ones that handle most, if not all of transactions, that involve money. To ensure that your records and transactions are secure, your data is secured in a centralized database that only authorized personnel are authorized to access.

Blockchain, on the other hand, promises to decentralize data in such a way that there would not be a single processor that would be handling it. For example, instead of having one or a couple of servers storing data for an insurance, everyone that is connected to a network will have access to insurance data.

That's right – this means that your data is going to be shared among a great number of people that needs to agree on its integrity.

Why Decentralize Data?

Think of the way you transact with any kind of business today – your information is stored in one place and is being processed and kept by only one institution. When you analyze the possibilities of having your most important data kept and processed by a single body, you get an idea that there are quite a number of unfortunate things that may happen. If that institution gets hacked, then all your important data is stolen in a one fell swoop. An institution, which is manned by people, can be prone to human error – one miscalculation or misreported transaction can cause serious repercussions. Also, organizations are prone to corruption – it's always easy for any bank or insurance firm to swindle the money out of their clients and the culprit will never be found again.

Blockchain's goal is to make sure that data and transactions that are done online are accurate and secure by removing the need for one type of organization to store one type of data. For example, if you're going to buy a house, you will need to find all the necessary data about the property that you are looking to buy. These days, you will need to talk to the current owner of the house and verify the details that he provides you through other sources, such as town records, previous owners, and so on. By decentralizing information, you will be able to trust that all the information you managed to gather are not tampered, since there is a group of people that are not interested in your deal that can guarantee you that your data is correct. In effect, you are assured that there is no safety hazard that has been intentionally kept from you.

Another one of blockchain's main thrusts is to take out the middlemen in your transactions – instead of having to go to Paypal or PayTM to send or collect money, your transaction will be processed instead in such a way that your data is encrypted and stored in a network of computers. The participants in this network can be anyone, and they each have a copy of your transaction (encrypted, of course), so that you won't need to need a payment firm to store your data. If you need to pull up a copy of that transaction, then it would be easy for you to retrieve it from the network as well. Even if one computer on the network crashed, there are still plenty of ways for you to retrieve your data. Also, since there are a lot of people that have evidence of how your transaction went through, you will be able to get proof if something went wrong. Since data is synchronized among participants, you have a record of all steps of transactions and there is no single network user that can make changes to your data without leaving a permanent track that everyone can easily trace.

With that simple example, you can see that blockchain promises to eliminate the three major issues that most people in the world who has ever needed any type of paperwork is likely to experience:

1. Data error
2. Fraud
3. Data misinterpretation

Bitcoin vs Blockchain

You might have heard of bitcoins, and you might have also heard of the terms blockchain and bitcoin being used interchangeably. However, these two are entirely different things. A bitcoin serves as a cryptocurrency – it has an assigned value (just like money), and is transferred securely from one person to another, thanks to blockchain. You can think of blockchain as a software that is used to record transactions, including the ones that involve bitcoins.

Chapter 2:

How Blockchain Works

In the last chapter, you have an idea of what blockchain can do for you once it is implemented across industries. However, you may be thinking that the entire idea is still so vast. In this chapter, you will learn the basics of blockchain, and how grasp why it is doable across businesses that you deal with on a daily basis.

By design, a blockchain is a structure made with data that makes up a digital ledger, which is not managed by any central authority. Its goal is to make sure that the digital hyper-ledger is distributed across a vast network of independent users to make sure that it maintains its integrity.

What Makes up a Blockchain?

Every blockchain is made up of three crucial parts:

1. The Block

When a transaction enters the hyper ledger, a block is created. Essentially, a block records the time, the size, and the event that triggers a particular event in a blockchain.

Take note that not every blockchain are created to record or keep a record of how a cryptocurrency. However, all blockchains do record what happens to a token or cryptocurrency. You can think of it just like how you would record every activity that you do. When you assign a value to a particular data, then you can think of ways how that data can be evaluated later on.

2. The Chain

The chain is a hash that connects a block to another one, and through math, you can chain them together. Because they are glued together through a particular key (or hash, for that matter), you can keep in mind that blocks in a blockchain are secured. The hashes that are used in a blockchain are made using information available in a previous block, and serves as a fingerprint. Because of that data, you know which block comes first in a sequence of events.

Why do blockchains use hashes? While block chaining, as a concept, is relatively new to every industry that it may affect, hashing is actually already a known concept. Hashing, as an innovation created 30 years ago, is created in such a way that a mathematical algorithm can be used in order to protect a particular data, just like how passwords work. Since they are encrypted and can be manufactured in such a way that there is a unique combination of data for every block that can enter a blockchain, it is extremely difficult to guess and alter. Since there is only one possible hash that can link two blocks together, changing it will also make it extremely easy for anyone to determine where a change in a blockchain happened.

3. The Network

The network is made up of full nodes, or computers that run the algorithm producing the hashes, which makes the blockchain secure. Every node in the system contains all the transactions that ever entered the blockchain, which makes it a complete ledger.

These nodes are scattered all over the world and can be operated by anyone who has a computer. Take note that it can take a lot of resources to run a node on your own, that's why people whose computers belong to this network receive some incentives. The reward

The ledger is composed of blocks of data, which is encrypted by a hashed key, which fit transactions that comes after or before it. When you put these blocks together (or chain them), you create a blockchain.

When you combine all these factors together, you will get a blockchain, which looks like this:

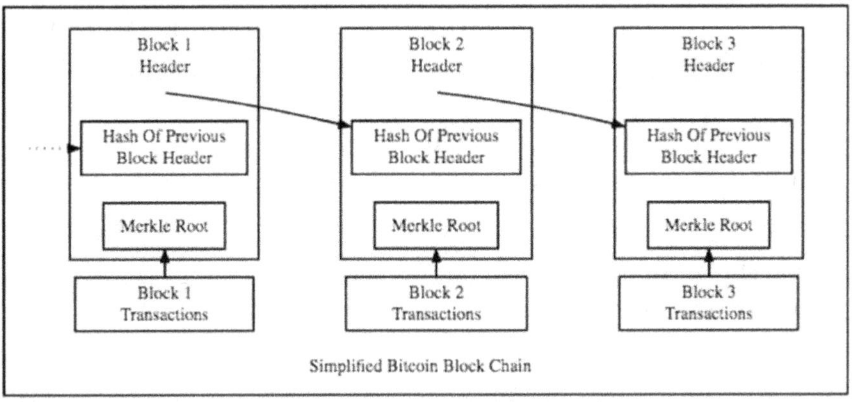

Simplified Bitcoin Block Chain

Exchanging Values on Blockchain

You now get the idea that blockchains are created to keep data. Within the same vein, you can also think of it as a way to exchange values.

Think of every currency that you have ever used – just like paper money, there are certain data that you have that you can exchange for something else, whether it is tangible or not.

When you think of value, people over a community assign a particular worth to anything that exists, and you can exchange something for another based on the rate that is assigned to it. In a blockchain, you can perform a similar exchange, as long as the "currency" can be swapped for something else within the system. While on a blockchain, you can enter contracts, make purchases, vote, or even contribute to the Internet of Things. Of course, all your transactions are recorded securely, so you can make sure that everything is in order.

Distributed Consensus

How does any blockchain make sure that every transaction is secured? The answer to this is consensus, wherein agreement within the blockchain network must exist in order for a block entry to be added to the chain.

Why is this important? The reason is simple – without agreement, it would be easy for anyone within the network to add or delete any data on the chain. At the very same time, the blockchain system is established in such a way that everybody knows that it would be vulnerable to outsider attack – everybody who is already using this system knows that it would be prone to hacking.

Bitcoins, for example, are currently known to have value to the point that they can actually be exchanged for goods and services. Just like real money, the economics to which it belongs to requires it to perform with specific requirements – it needs to have consistency, threat and failure models, as we well as scalability in order for it to perform as currency.

Because it can be exchanged as it is assigned a value, the bitcoin system operates in such a way that everybody assumes that there will always be somebody that would want to corrupt the system of the blockchains that it belongs to in order to change the history of trading in order to steal bitcoins.

The blockchain prevents this by using a model called "proof or work". This model is created to solve the problem of making sure that every detail that you are looking at in a blockchain is never changed by the people within the network or outside it. In order for this to happen, an algorithm of consensus is used in every network.

However, it may seem that having to solve a math problem in order for everyone to meet the consensus (producing the "proof or work") may take a long time. What about financial transactions done online that needs a speedy process in order for exchange to take place? When speedy transactions are needed, one can opt to have a different way of reaching the consensus within the network. You will learn about this later.

Would Blockchains Prevent Double Spending?

Double spending happens when one person spends his bitcoin balance in more than one transaction. This, of course, is a major concern in every digital transaction.

To briefly answer this issue, a blockchain, by itself, is not capable of preventing double spending. However, blockchain makes sure that all the transactions that used the bitcoin balance in question are confirmed. Once these transactions are verified, they cannot be changed anymore. Moreover, they will also be posted among the members of the network.

How will blockchains handle double spending then? If there are two separate transactions that aim to spend the same bitcoin, then the blockchain would reject both transactions in order to prevent the bitcoin from two different ends. This way, the owner of the bitcoin will be forced to only spend a value once. This solves the issue of double spending.

For example, if Person A wants to spend 5 bitcoins and send it to Person B, that transaction is automatically recorded as a block, and then issued a specific hash in order for it to be locked in a blockchain. Now, if Person A would want to process another transaction and use the very same bitcoins to buy something from Person C, the network would immediately nullify this transaction. If Person A would want to check if the transaction is done right, he would also have the ability to download the blockchain and check for any mistakes in the process.

Moreover, blocks also have the ability to change states, depending on the transactions that are to be done. For example, if Person A have 100 bitcoins and he would want to send 40 bitcoins to Person B, the blocks are going to change in such a way that Person A will have 60 bitcoins, and B has 40 additional bitcoins.

Mining

At this point, you are already aware that it is possible for you to earn some compensation when you are part of the blockchain network. Mining, in essence, is the reason why every node within a network is capable of cooperating with each other to reach a consensus, despite having a system wherein nobody knows each other.

How does one mine in a blockchain? One process used is bitcoin mining, wherein a node in a network should serve two purposes: to confirm a particular transaction by exerting computation power (called effort) to a block, and to create new bitcoins for every block that is confirmed. When successful, a node will be able to then choose the most recent block's header and then insert it as a hash. Afterwards, the node will then solve the problem of proof of work. Once it finds the solution, the block will finally be added to the blockchain and will be spread throughout the network.

You might be curious about the Proof of Work (otherwise known as PoW) – what kind of task does a miner do in order to earn compensation for adding a block. In essence, PoW is simply a type of data that can be difficult to produce, mainly because it has energy and time costs, but it makes it easy for anyone to verify that a specific node has met certain requirements. To produce a PoW, you will need to enter a random process – if you want to generate proof of work without entering the process that is required by a blockchain, you will need to do a lot of trial and error to produce it, which generally would require you to spend more time and electricity. In essence, having to spend too many resources in order to get the compensation that nodes get when they produce PoW will make no sense since you will need to outspend resources and get less in return.

One type of Proof of Work system that you might encounter is the HashCash, which is widely used in bitcoin transactions. This system does what most mining systems do – in order for a node to actually get compensation in bitcoins, they will need to take a certain block's data, and apply a math formula in it, turning it into something else when it is placed in the network. The result is that the data that is collected through mining becomes a hash, making the transaction unique and indecipherable.

Now, here is where the real fun begins – every time you turn a block into a hash, you get bitcoins, which is a good value in return for the work that you have done. However, turning blocks is not that easy – while computers can be great at encrypting data into hashes, the result should follow a certain format in order to be rendered valid.

Summary of How Blockchain Works

At this point, you are already aware of how every component of the blockchain works. You are also aware that every node in the blockchain network work together in order to determine the validity of all transactions in the blockchain and keep the data within it intact. However, you also know that while every node or computer in the blockchain network needs to cooperate, there is also a notion of distrust – while everybody has a copy of a block and all the blocks that came before it, everybody also operates in an assumption that blockchains are very prone to being attacked. That is why every block in the blockchain is encrypted.

Every person in the blockchain network that has a machine dedicated to verifying blocks by producing Proof of Work is also incentivized – in exchange for evaluating data (and spending resources doing so), every block that has been evaluated yields bitcoins, which can be exchanged online for goods and services.

When everything goes well, all layers of transactions that are recorded on a blockchain are final and irreversible. Even attempting to hack the system is impractical, because it means having to spend too many resources than gaining something from it.

Chapter 3:

History of Blockchain and Bitcoin

How did blockchain become the innovation that we know today? When you trace back its roots, blockchain is that technology that made the bitcoin currency secure. Without the blockchain technology, the bitcoin probably would not have become one of the most lucrative mode of exchange today.

How Did Everything Happen?

The idea of using chains of blocks in such a way that they are secured using cryptography has been around as early as 1991. The first application is the incorporation of Merklee trees, which are essentially pieces of data that are encrypted and linked together according to value or chronology. Just like blockchains today, Merklee trees are designed to create an efficient and secure method of verifying data that is stored in large structures. Think of encrypted data in servers, for example – organizations today can easily retrieve and store data in such a way that no outsider can access and steal information.

The Mystery of the First Blockchain

The blockchain, as you know now, was first introduced in 2008 by Satoshi Nakamoto. In 2009, it was used as the component that made the bitcoin, which is the first digital currency that is managed and distributed without a decentralized system. What makes the introduction of both the bitcoin and the blockchain is that it is actually created by an unknown entity – the name Satoshi Nakamoto is actually a pseudonym, and up to date, no one knows who this person really is. Satoshi Nakamoto released the bitcoin and the blockchain through an open-source program, wherein the currency is exchanged using a peer-to-peer network. The first receiver of a bitcoin transaction was Hal Finney, who received 10 bitcoins. Satoshi Nakamoto was the first to mine bitcoins by verifying the first block, which has a reward of 50 bitcoins.

At this point you may begin to think this: isn't the peer-to-peer system designed to fail, because people are not cooperative in the first place? Just think of the torrent system, where everybody has access to an uploaded file. While everybody has the means to download the file, not everybody is doing their responsibility to seed these files in order for other people to be able to have access to the files.

This is where the blockchain innovation truly shines – it solved the problem of the traditional P2P system by offering an economic incentive to those who are willing to follow the bitcoin protocol, which is for the people participating to verify blocks.

Determining the Bitcoin's Value

During the early days of bitcoin, its value was determined through bitcointalk, or forums that are dedicated in discussing how much the digital currency should be valued at. While you may have knowledge that a bitcoin has a great value, one of the early real-world transactions involved 10000 BTC, which was then used to buy 2 Papa John's pizza.

How is the bitcoin valued nowadays? It might be a bit difficult to grasp why something that only exists digitally actually has value. The answer is actually very simple – it is rather difficult to produce and has limited supply. To date, the maximum number of bitcoins in circulation is only 21 million – by capping the amount of bitcoins to this amount makes it known to everyone that not everyone can have it.

Just like anything that has value, bitcoins can be useful – you just have to realize how it can be valuable to your life. Take for example the internet and the telephone – when they were first introduced, people have no idea how these inventions could be used to make their lives better. However, people have taken notice of their properties – they can make communication faster. The same goes for bitcoins – since this currency is borderless and makes almost no use of intermediaries, they are great in being exchanged for goods and services. All that the bitcoin and the blockchain needs is for people to use it in order to have very apparent usefulness. The more people use it, the more valuable they become.

Pricing the Bitcoin

Just like most currencies, the actual price of a bitcoin is not equal to its value – its exchange rate is determined by its competitiveness in the market using the laws of price and demand. When you think about it, it is almost similar to how gold is valuated – it is not as easy to manufacture as paper money, but since there are a lot of people that would like to use it for exchanges, its value becomes greater.

The Luno Exchange, which is considered as the stock market exchange of bitcoin, sets the price of bitcoin for a particular time and place. Just like stocks, Luno is not the sole body that determines the price of the bitcoin – those that engage in trading it through buying and selling are the ones that do.

Just like in stock market, the price of the bitcoin is determined at the amount that buyers willingly would shell out for the future value of the bitcoin. When buyers think that bitcoin will have much more value in the future, say 10 years from now, they are more likely to pay for bitcoins now.

Volatility

How volatile is the bitcoin? Just like most products and industries that are being traded in the stock market, you can expect its price to swing wildly on a daily basis. In 2013, it is lauded by Forbes to be the best investment to make, but one year later, it is considered as the worst.

It is also important to consider that the bitcoin market is relatively small compared to the market that other industries trade in. Because of this, the price of the bitcoin is still considered to be extremely volatile. However, as more merchants make use of the bitcoin as a legitimate currency for exchange, the more stable this digital money becomes.

Blockchain's Growth

Blockchain, as a software, changed according to the need of industries for a smarter data-keeping. During its early days, the size of the block is mere 2 MB – even smaller than the size of most of the .mp3 files you might have. However, like most successful programs in the world, the capacity of a block has increased, making it more adaptable by more industries. In 2014, the bitcoin blockchain file size can reach 20 Gbs. In 2015, it has become 30 Gb.

When you look back at the history of the bitcoin, you will realize that bitcoin has been a real game changer thanks to the introduction of the blockchain. This technology single-handedly solved the bitcoin's major security flaws, such as double spending, possible wallet theft, and time jacking (you'll find out more about this later).

The blocks of the blockchain made it possible for additional transactions, but the old data is plainly immutable. That means that in a blockchain, one can only add new blocks, but it is virtually impossible for someone to change the old ones. At the same time, the Proof of Work concept that incentivizes those who are willing to verify data also allowed new transactions to be added to a blockchain in a faster and more efficient manner – higher transaction fees or incentives make it possible to provide PoW more quickly, thus, allowing for transactions to be done quickly.

Chapter 4:

Benefits of Blockchain Technology

How does the blockchain technology aim to improve different industries that it affects? It all boils down to the level of control that everybody who experiences this technology enjoys. All industries need to make sure that data is secure and can be easily traced, without having to sacrifice precision and speed of transfer. At the same time, industries also need to have a method of securities and exchange that doesn't cost a lot. Blockchain offers all these by offering the following:

Transparency

The blockchain technology holds the promise that every detail in every transaction will be transparent, thanks to decentralization of data. In blockchain, all participants have a copy of every data, which drastically reduces the risk of hidden data changes and fraud. Because the history of every data can be traced from numerous points, you will not need having an intermediary that holds all the information. At the same time, this will effectively reduce or even remove counterparty risks and fraud.

Take the diamond industry for example, which is in high risk of fraud and corruption. You barely have any idea on what happens in between mining and delivery of the supply to the consumers, and that gray area to consumers like you makes you think that there are possible incidents of fraud that happened in between. However, if everyone will have a copy of all transactions that are happening from the moment the gem is mined, then you can be sure that you are getting the right cut and clarity without anyone bloating its value.

Removal of Intermediaries

Most of the transactions that you do, online or not, needs an intermediary. This third party to every transaction makes it a point that each party in a deal fulfills the obligation by tracking and storing data involved in the transaction. However, having an intermediary has possible risks. Since intermediaries bridge two different parties in a transaction, it is possible for an intermediary's system to fail, which brings a halt to any deal that they may be mediating. You might have experienced this numerous times when you attempt to make online transactions, only to find out that your purchase cannot go through because PayPal is down.

Intermediaries are also extremely prone to external attacks. When a service such as an online banking system is successfully hacked, you can probably imagine that thousands, if not millions, of their customers' data are also at risk. By removing intermediaries, people are not likely to suffer potential identity theft due to an attack to a third party.

Since different businesses are bound to rely on the blockchain, instead of an intermediary-provided data, it will be easier and less costly for any person to avail services in the future. Because service providers will have direct access to a blockchain that contains important details that they need to verify, they will not have to run personal data through an external party in order to approve any transaction. This makes services more seamless. Imagine this – you can make loans without having to deal with a credit verifier to get approved!

Decentralization

Decentralization of data is one of the main strengths of the blockchain technology. When information is centralized, everybody will have legal access to needed data. That means that there is not one company or organization that holds all relevant data – because blockchain works like a Google Sheet that everybody can see but not edit, every transaction is also transparent to all parties. By decentralizing data, you do not need anyone to serve as a confirming party on whether transactions should push through or not, making services more efficient and transparent.

Trust

The blockchain is bound to change the way you trust – because you can be secure that the entire system has the right security measures, you can stop relying on the more traditional methods of trust, such as banking systems and security servers.

Security

While everybody has access to data stored in blocks, the proof of work concept that powers the entire blockchain is designed to make the entire system secure. That means that it is designed in such a way that it is impossible to be tampered with and that all transactions within it are immutable.

Wide Range of Uses

The blockchain is not just applicable to crypto economics (the type of economics that the use of bitcoin has created). It is applicable to almost every industry that you can think of, which includes the government, finance, real estate, and so on. As long as an industry or organization needs to make sure that its data is secure, then blockchain can be used.

Reduced Costs

Blockchain is created to make transactions efficient, and in the long run, the efficiency that it offers drastically cuts down resources needed to process any business.

Chapter 5:

Disadvantages and Dangers of Using Blockchain Technology

While blockchain seems to be the most sensible direction to take when it comes to improving data security and efficiency when doing transactions, there are certain risks in adapting the blockchain technology. At this point, it is important to acknowledge that the blockchain technology is a work-in-progress – while it is definitely promising, there are still a lot of areas that needs work.

Lack of Privacy

Security may be one of the greatest strengths of the blockchain, thanks to its ability to make sure that all transactions are immutable. However, it also means that your transactions are transmitted all over the world.

Take the bitcoin, for example. While the bitcoin allows you to send currency to another person anonymously, it doesn't mean that your transactions cannot be traced back to you. Owners of transactions are being hidden by pseudonyms, but it can be generally easy for anyone to pull up your transactions. The reason is simple – your transactions are spread over a network, where everybody has a copy of all transactions that you have made.

Security Concerns

Because the blockchain is used for crypto economics and are slowly being rolled out to different industries, it is one of the technologies that are most prone to attacks. While solutions are being developed to combat possible attacks against existing blockchains, there are still a number of security concerns that institutions need to think about before fully implementing the blockchain technology.

While blockchains make it impossible to change a verified transaction, it is important to take note that attackers can still hack blocks that are yet to be added to the blockchain. When you think about this major security loophole, you can think of a number of ways this can be done through social engineering, distributed denial of service, or introduction of a malware. It is also be possible to steal bitcoin wallets, which are unencrypted and can be accessed by passwords.

Immutability may be the strongest asset of the blockchain, but it is also important to recognize that it also welcomes new cyberthreats, such as interception and backdoor programs that are made to create a man-in-the-middle attack. Until these possible threats are addressed before this technology is rolled out to end users, it would be easy to say that this technology should not be available to everybody just yet.

No Centralized Control

Once you adopt the blockchain technology, there is no institution that is tasked to watch over your transactions and police anyone that might be trying to break the rules. Since there is no intermediary in the blockchain system, you are empowered to make decisions that will allow you to transact in any way that you want, as long as it is verifiable. However, that also means that there is no one telling you that you might be doing a transaction that is not beneficial to you. At the same time, you also can't hold one organization liable when a transaction has gone awry.

Risk of 51% Attack

As you may have observed, the blockchain is ruled by the majority – in order for a transaction to be considered valid, it has to be approved by 51% of the nodes that are participating in the blockchain network. This means that it is hypothetically possible for an entity to gain control of what blocks should be added in a blockchain as long as they will have control of the majority of the nodes.

What will this mean? In the event that a 51% attack happens, the one that is controlling the majority will have the power to decline any transactions that are to be added to the blockchain. They will also have the power to reverse recent transactions. However, it will be impossible to make any changes on old blocks.

Cost

While blockchain promises to cut costs when it comes to processing transactions and keeping data, it doesn't mean that it is free. Those that are participating in the network needs to spend electricity and computational power in order to validate transactions. At the same time, data storage also means that those that are maintaining a blockchain needs to invest on storage devices in order to save all transactions stored in a blockchain.

Scalability Issues

Since the blockchain is a fairly new innovation, one of the issues that it faces is scalability. At this point, technologies are still being developed in order to store larger transactions in a block. Bitcoin, for example, is currently limited at the size of 1Mb per block, which caps the number of transactions that can be made using this cryptocurrency at 7 transactions per second (tsp). Visa, on the other hand, was able to already scale at 2000 tsps.

Reputation and Trust

While the blockchain offers a lot of promise to consumers all over the world, it is still not as well-reputable as traditional and centralized organizations that are designed to handle trust. While trust industries such as the banking sector have opened themselves to using the blockchain industry, they are not yet welcoming the idea of using cryptocurrency to replace the fiat currency or paper money.

Regulation and Integration

Blockchain, like other new technological infrastructures, face regulatory issues – to date, several organizations are having a hard time adopting this technology due to lack of legal framework that will support its functions. Among of the major issues that it faces is its immutable nature and its decentralization – many industries are still doing the hard job of having a legal framework that deals with mistakes in transactions that cannot be deleted or changed, as well as the legal implications of data disclosure as evidence.

The Takeaway

While blockchain is offering solutions that everybody craves for when it comes to accessibility and data security, it is important to remember that this is still a man-made creation – it is not going to be perfect, and the applications and utility that you can enjoy are only as good as the code that it is written on. Since all programs running on a blockchain are still going to be created by a person or a group of people, it does not mean that they are going to be flawless or even less malicious than the apps that are available on the market right now. You need to expect that there are some programs that are going to be written for the blockchain network that may not run as intended, and mistakes can be exploited for an attack.

Blockchain, as of the moment, is enjoyable at your own risk. However, blockchain is always about freedom, which has always come with a responsibility.

Chapter 6:

Blockchain and the Finance Industry

One of the industries that will largely benefit from the blockchain industry is finance. With the adoption of blockchain, it is a safe assumption that it will be easier for everyone to deal with financial transactions since data is already decentralized, making transactions easier to verify and approve. While enjoying better transparency, consumers and industries are also bound to enjoy lower transaction costs. In effect, everyone can look forward to enhanced transaction speed without having to spend extra. It's an obvious win-win situation between companies and their consumers.

Better Currency Transfer

If you have experienced sending or receiving money from abroad, one of the major challenges that you might have faced is having to face a long processing time. Let's face it – overseas money transfer has become increasingly difficult, despite the technology that is available now. The reason is simple – with the increased risks associated with fraud, terrorism, money laundering, and other crimes that involve money, banks all over the world need to add layers of security in order to prevent money that flows through them go to these activities.

Scrutiny has always been part of currency transfer, making transactions infuriatingly long and tedious. This effectively slows down the transferring of certain values from one company or country to another. With the blockchain's promise that all transactions are more secure and that no organization or individual can change data that are entered into a transaction, value transfer is expected to be done in a more timely manner. In time, you can expect these transfers to be done in an instant.

More Efficient Layers of Authentication

One of blockchains offerings is to ensure that transactions are secure by making sure that its end users are able to prove their ownership of transaction. This is spot on for the finance industry. By making an entire network of computers capable of verifying all transactions involved in a transaction, businesses have a way of verifying the legitimacy of every purchase or exchange made over a network. At the same time, end users will be secure that nothing on their data is changed.

Share Trading

Today, the finance industry relies on correspondent banking, or the practice on relying on partners in order to process a transaction on behalf of a customer's main bank. This way, the finance industry is able to make tons of profit.

One of the services that correspondent banking offers is transfer of value or currency in locations wherein a bank cannot. However, this presents some issues. When a value is transferred using these intermediaries, transparency is lost – you barely have knowledge of what happens in between the value transfers. Because lack of transparency brings transactions into question, banks are now cutting ties with their intermediaries.

Blockchain, on the other hand, is a solution that the finance industry may find to be extremely handy when it comes to addressing transparency issues. Instead of having to rely on middlemen to handle transactions, this technology allows share trading, or the transfer of ownership from one person to another. This not only removes issues of transparency that having to pass currency from one middleman to another until the value reaches its intended goal, but also solves the issue of cost that arises when institutions rely on correspondent banking.

The Update That We Need

Most of the processes that several institutions in the world of commerce is outdated. Because people still tend to rely on fiat currency in order to process exchanges, they tend to forget that commerce has gone digital already. Many of the monetary transactions that are done today are done over the internet. However, what will happen when the middlemen that makes online transactions happen are gone for a day? If payment processors that exist online go down for one day, the entire internet commerce goes down as well. People would need to line up to their banks in order to shop for goods and services. Now that is just inefficient.

Instead of having to rely on manual banking and exchange in the absence of payment processors, people would be able to still make financial transactions if they adapt more agile technologies. That is exactly what the blockchain technology offers. By making consumers empowered to make transactions and ensure their validity without having to rely on a third party outfit or manual paperwork, exchanges become more secure and efficient.

The Finance Industry's Current Use of the Blockchain

Is blockchain already made available to the finance sector? The answer is a resounding yes – mainstream companies are already starting to invest on this technology and slowly adopting it into their processes. Take Visa, for example – this industry giant has already started testing interbank payment systems that make use of blockchains. Mastercard is also starting to adopt blockchain when it comes to making online payments faster.

Samsung has also started partnering with fintech corporations in creating its own credit card system, which is designed to usher mobile banking and also instill brand loyalty to their consumers.

Chapter 7:

Blockchain and Industries Other Than Finance

What other industries will be affected by the blockchain? Probably every industry that you can think of – decentralization of data has wide use, which can be adopted by almost every business out there.

Identity Management and Digital Identities

Every business relies on people – all stores that aim to make a profit needs to interact with real people in order to make sure that an actual exchange can take place. In the digital age where it is rather easy to create virtual identities, it is important for businesses to make sure that they are dealing with real people that are actually capable of meeting their end of the bargain.

You, the consumer, also has the same need – you want to make sure that whenever you whip out your credit card, you are actually dealing with a legitimate business that will be able to deliver the goods and services that you are paying for. In 2016 alone, 1.61 billion people made online transactions, and you are probably expecting this number to grow in this digital age.

Because digital identities are needed to actually process transactions, these identities are very prone to attack. Blockchain ensures that digital identities do not get stolen by locking them. That means that the network would need to verify all changes done on a digital identity, and at the same time, blockchain users will also have the means to securely verify their identity when they perform transactions online.

Digital Voting

Yes, blockchains can change the way you elect your officials, but in a good way. With blockchains, you have the confidence that your votes will not magically disappear or counted towards someone that you definitely do not want to be in office.

Elections, especially national elections, demand the ultimate security technology has to offer. Current elections pose some issues – data servers can be hacked, and offline elections do not offer transparency. With the introduction of blockchain to the electoral system, these possible compromises can be avoided. At the same time, voters can also enjoy a few add-ons, such as the possibility of online voting.

Healthcare and Medical Records

The healthcare system's methods of handling data are one of the most vulnerable methods when it comes to information security. Face it – healthcare needs some update when it comes to data exchange, billing management, and maintaining the integrity of research materials.

With the introduction of blockchain to the medical world, risks that the healthcare industry can be drastically reduced. Not only will this industry prevent data breaches due to ransomware and hacking, but it will also be easy for patients to verify and submit their medical records as well as other pertinent data such as social security numbers and medicard data. It will also be easier for pharmaceutical and health researchers to maintain the integrity of clinical trials and research. As a result, the world can enjoy more efficient healthcare transactions with medical facilities being able to enjoy more reliable data management.

Cloud Storage

You might be enjoying the benefits of cloud storage today – you have the ability to access your files anywhere in the world using any device that has internet connectivity. However, you also know that cloud storages today, such as Dropbox, Microsoft Azure, and AWS comes with high cost. When security breach or data failure happens, you might have to spend more than you should.

Centralized data storage comes with expenditure, thanks to the cost of physical server, networking devices, and electricity. Companies that offer data storage services spend billions of dollars every year just updating and managing their services. Because this cost is passed on to the consumer, you are paying a high price in order to avail their services. However, this doesn't even mean that your data is secure or not prone to failure.

Decentralizing the cloud storage could work wonders for every person who uses it because it makes their data verifiable and tamper-proof. It works great for people who store sensitive data online or those who need to keep track of data changes they have made to their own files. At the same time, a publicly available blockchain of stored data could also get rid of middlemen. As a result, everybody can enjoy fast and economical data storage facility on the cloud, with less security issues.

Chapter 8:

Ethereum, Smart Contracts, and Decentralized Applications

Now that you are aware of blockchains and bitcoins, it's time for you to learn a different type of blockchain called Ethereum.

At this point, you may think that blockchain is a bit impossible for you to grasp because you cannot imagine how this technology could apply to your everyday transactions. All the benefits that you have read in the previous chapters may seem a bit hard to grasp because it might seem impossible for the world today to actually build technologies that would make all of them possible. This is where Ethereum enters.

What is Ethereum?

Ethereum is an open-source platform that makes it possible for developers to create and use decentralized applications to several industries. By decentralizing apps, you will have full control of the data in everything that you do online – as an owner of something that you upload online, you should have the ability to know what is going on when you send any data and have control over it.

Take Google Docs for example – you are storing data over a third party that takes charge of making your files accessible online. While it is free and convenient to use, you do not have any idea what's going on when you store a piece of information on a cloud. That means you do not have any idea if any document that you uploaded have been accessed by someone or has been changed while it is in the internet cloud.

At the same time, third parties, such as Google and Apple, take charge of what apps you can use in order to do anything on your devices. You might have noticed that there are only a limited number of apps that you could download.

Ethereum wants to change that status quo – by making it possible to develop applications that can be used on any device, you will no longer have to rely on an app store that displays a limited number of applications that Android or Apple chose to support. You will instead get services from a service provider online that is not controlled by a single company. Because these services are also going to be governed by the blockchain, you do not have to worry if the stuff that you are going to do using them are going to be changed or stolen – your activities are still going to be stored in blocks, which means that they are immutable and can be easily verified.

Difference Between Bitcoin and Ethereum

Is Ethereum any different from the Bitcoin? Yes, at a certain point – both technologies make it possible for transactions to be available on a public network that operates a blockchain, but they differ in purpose. Bitcoin's purpose is to make it possible for you to transfer money using a digital currency. Ethereum, on the other hand, is focused in creating and running decentralized applications.

What you can mine in Ethereum, should your computer operate as a node in its network, is called the Ether. Just like in the bitcoin blockchain, verified transactions in an Ethereum are compensated, but with a different cryptocurrency called Ether. Just like bitcoins, Ethers have an exchangeable value, but are often used by developers working in this blockchain when they need to spend for services or transaction fees within an Ethereum network.

Decentralized Applications

Decentralized applications, or dapps, are among the most amazing ideas born out of the blockchain technology. Dapps are powered by smart contracts (you will know more about this later) and are set to run without Google Play or Apple backing them up. They are independent of app giants, and are dependent on the network for verification of online tasks that are channeled to them.

Without having to rely on third party services, dapps are starting to change the way people are handling day-to-day transactions that they do online by replacing traditional online apps that used to control the market. For example, people can now go crowdfunding without having to deal with Kickstarter or any similar platforms, thanks to WeiFund. By having a browser that supports Weifund 3.0, you can start a crowdfunding campaign or contribute. This new platform does not accept cash yet though – all donations must be digital currency. Weifund also has its own wallet system that is also powered by the blockchain, making all transactions secure and easy to verify.

Another exciting dapp is the Vevue project, which aims to enable all users to submit videos of different locations for everyone to enjoy to power the Google Street View. To participate, all you need is to answer video requests from Viveo using your smartphone. The best part is that you can earn bitcoins using your contributions.

The lending industry is also being changed by the dapp, with the introduction of applications that allow people to make loans, even on hard-to-reach areas. 4G Capital made this possible may granting small businesses to access credit. Donors that are using this dapp can also send funds to beneficiaries through digital currency. This means that the grass roots finally have access to this important business aspect.

Dapps may also start to change the way people do social media. Right now, there is a prototype of a microblogging platform call Eth-Tweet, which is an application that is very similar to Twitter. However, since there is no single body that tells people what they can publish, only the author has the ability to remove what he or she publishes.

Apart from being tamper-proof and secure, dapps are never bound to suffer from downtime. The logic here is extremely simple – since they are not powered by a third party's physical server and employees, they will continue running unless someone takes down the entire Ethereum network that runs it, which is virtually impossible to do. That means that everything that you do in a dapp will never be lost.

Smart Contracts

A smart contract is essentially the code that is able to facilitate any transaction that you can run on an Ethereum network, which includes the exchange of currency, content, shares, or anything that has value. You can think of smart contracts as computers that operate on their own that triggers events when a specific condition is met.

Because a blockchain manages a smart contract, they are bound to run exactly as they intended. That means that once it starts running, all data that enters it cannot be censored, stolen, changed, or be interfered by a third party.

What kinds of operations can a smart contract do? In the Ethereum blockchain, your imagination is your only limit – any developer can write a code that can do any kind of operation possible within the computing world. That means that with smart contracts, you are bound to have software experiences that are not possible before.

Chapter 9:

Technical Guide to the Blockchain

At this point, you now have a full grasp of the basics – you know what you can expect from the blockchain as an end user. Now, could you be a part of the network that powers a blockchain? This chapter will teach you how you can start being part of this system.

In this chapter, you will learn how the blockchain technology works in a more technical manner. The previous chapters helped you learn how it is supposed to work, but if you want to participate as a miner or a developer in an Ethereum, this chapter will introduce you to the core technicalities that you need to learn in order to start working on a blockchain.

Technical Guide to How the Blockchain Works

The blockchain works the way that it does because of the following properties:

Hashing

Hashing is the method of creating an output of a given length from an input of any possible length. The bitcoin makes use of the SHA-256, which means that it creates a 256-bit output out of a data of any length. As explained earlier, hashing allows the entire system which data points out to the next block.

Moreover, the hashes allow the blockchain system to remain immutable.

Signatures

Just like in real life, signatures in a blockchain allows the system to know that a transaction is verified. Like the very nature of your personal signature, blockchain signatures should have the ability to be non-forgeable. At the same time, it gives the block the nature of non-repudiation. This means that once you assign your signature to a specific transaction, you should not be able to take that action back or even claim that someone signed it for you.

Signatures in real world have flaws – no matter how intricate a signature is, someone out there will still be able to forge it. Moreover, it is extremely difficult for anyone to verify if a signature is authentic. That means that the signatures that you attach using your hand are not reliable nor efficient.

Thanks to cryptography, you can make use of a private key that proves that you allow a transaction to happen from your end. At the same time, you can only decrypt information that makes use of your private key. It is also impossible for you to deny transactions that make use of your key since they can only be traced back to you.

Proof of Work

Proof of Work is the way coordination and consensus is reached in the blockchain system. Since numerous people and machines are operating to keep a blockchain in order, you need to make sure that everything is coordinated and can be easily verified.

Zero Knowledge Proofs

Zero knowledge proof, or simple ZKP, makes it possible for you to prove that you know something without having to tell that person what that knowledge is. This is what makes transactions private in a blockchain.

For a ZKP to actually work, it has to meet the following conditions:

- Completeness – if you are telling something that is true, then a verifier should be able to prove that what you are saying is indeed true.
- Soundness – if you are telling something that is false, then the verifier should not be convinced that what you are saying is true
- Zero-knowledge – if you are going to say that something is true, the verifier should not be able to know that that something is.

Different blockchains may use different technologies to make ZKPs happen in their system, but the idea behind them remains the same. All these technologies make use of a truth that can be figured out by a certain computation without having to reveal the data that it is verifying.

What Happens to a Blockchain When Transactions are Added

When a transaction enters the blockchain, it becomes a block. However, people who are using the blockchain wants to make sure that all the data in this transaction remains intact – it should not be altered in any way once this particular event is recorded. For this reason, it is assigned a hash, or the chain, that cannot be decrypted in any way. When another event, or block, is added into the blockchain, a different key is assigned to connect the next block to the block that comes before it. This process is repeated, as long as there are events that follow the sequence.

Now, it does not mean that any transaction can just be added on the blockchain – the network needs to make sure that the transaction is allowable before it is considered a process that is worth adding to the entire ledger. Take a look at this diagram:

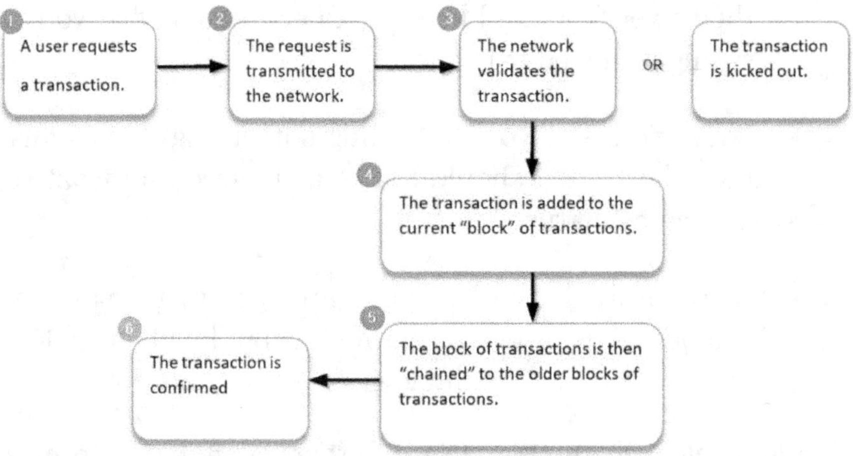

Looking at this image, you also get the idea that once a block is accepted as a valid transaction, it gets added as a permanent block into the blockchain. This means that this transaction is already made "public" to those that belong to this blockchain's network!

However, what makes your transaction within a blockchain also private? Remember that every blockchain is encrypted with a hash – that means that every person within the network can only see a bunch of characters that essentially describe your data in a mathematical way. Since they cannot see the nature of your transactions, nobody within the network will actually see the intention of your transactions. Without knowing that, they will not be able to determine what a transaction is about in a surface level. The only way to do that is to decrypt the hash, which is almost impossible to do using a single computer.

Hashing Transactions into Blocks

As mentioned earlier, hashing essentially turns a transaction into an encrypted data using all details that are within it. You can think of a hash as a combination for a lock – the more numbers it has, the harder it is to guess. Hashing essentially prevents anything on a block from being deciphered easily, making it almost impossible for anyone to know what a transaction is about.

When you hash a transaction into a block, you are essentially locking in all the data in that transaction and you turn that into an immutable record. The reason is simple: once you hash a transaction, you will never be able to convert it into its original version, which makes it a one-way encryption. When you are able to meet the conditions of a hash required for a blockchain that you want to mine, you turn a transaction into a block. The more people hashing a specific transaction, the faster a transaction can be turned into a block. In an essence, the "proof of work" that is required for any miner to produce is their share of the hashing the block, since it takes great computational effort to produce the hash that the blockchain requires. Right now, it takes an entire network about 10 minutes to "solve" a block using the SHA-256. You will recognize this type of hash when you see a hexadecimal value that contains 64 characters, such as 7f83b1657ff1fc53b92dc18148a1d65dfc2d4b1fa3d677284addd200126d9069.

Blockchain

When you successfully hashed a transaction into a block, and it is the first block in the blockchain, that specific block is termed the genesis block, or the block 0. All other blocks will reference it for the next transactions.

For example, these transactions happened over a bitcoin blockchain:

David receives 70 bitcoins

Sam receives 50 bitcoins

Sarah receives 10 bitcoins

When you turn these transactions into an encrypted value using the SHA-256 algorithm, you will get these results:

David receives 70 bitcoins:
55cd828ee40d78a9a945d3a087c4ee2424fd3e8fdfd29bfaa915
3d06f158f917

Sam receives 50 bitcoins:
b4b48a675d9837320adde11ee166845bc92744d850a3835895a
51cfd837e72bc

Sarah receives 10 bitcoins:

6cb6b9c49d9209d005e6d4299a9868a65e6a950710e13473ff2
309828241a5a3

Once these transactions are confirmed, they may be added to the public ledger as a block. If you are going to hash this proposed block using SHA-256, you should get this value: 2f4598cc8dff236bf4bd96a05580910dce4d905440ef92866a25
9fbec401048a.

Now, how would David, Sam, and Sarah keep track of the transaction that they performed? Simple: they have a private key (also encrypted) that will allow them to prove that they are the owner of the transaction and to keep track of what happens after they perform an exchange. This private key also serves as their signature that tells the blockchain community that they authorized the exchange to happen.

However, simply hashing this type of transaction to show this result is not enough to mine it successfully. For you to actually get this transaction into a block in a bitcoin blockchain, you would need to solve a mathematical puzzle which you can answer by adding some characters to a transaction, wherein you need to arrive at a particular output. Right now, you are required to create a hash that has eighteen zeroes (as of this writing) at the beginning of the hashed result before the bitcoin community renders your hash valid.

For that reason, you would need to collaborate with other miners to contribute to your hashing efforts, because it will take a long time for a single computer to "solve the puzzle". As of now, it takes approximately 10 minutes for a network of computers to produce the nonce (or number used only once), which is the hashed output needed to confirm a block. The nonce is what nodes are competing for in order to get compensation for hashing a block.

Now, once the above transaction's hash is solved (meaning you get the amount of zeros required for a specific blockchain that you want to work on), then it is considered to be an approved transaction. Now, when a second transaction comes up, it also needs to get hashed. Let's take this example as the second block, or the block 1:

David sends Sam 50 bitcoins:

Sam sends Sarah 10 bitcoins

When you hash these statements, they turn into this:

David sends Sam 50 bitcoins:
a1b9358354a05b5b568dd182ff17342243054340ca41b635273bd9280d8ee0bc

Sam sends Sarah 10 bitcoins:
ef76f7b14fb48ab78e00fbdfe1a62303cdedf48e6559526b81a3a8a1b342f6ad

When you hash these transactions together, they should yield this value:
d5805f3ad8a39378c1ff03084820d41858dfb394138e57a8064de2f5dd4c03c1

The second block of a blockchain, also known as the Block 1, would also need to contain the information available from the previous block in its hash. If you are going to take these two blocks together and hash them with a SHA-256 algorithm, you should be able to get this result:

cd58276bff695c0d207626bd62a18f642c9810a8403a6ba2dbf55b89cd426265

Again, in order for this to be turned into an approved block on a blockchain, miners should be able to create a hash that will have 18 zeroes in order for the block to be added to a blockchain.

Now, if you are going to add these specific transactions as a third block, or Block 2, you should get results like these:

Sam sends Sarah 20 bitcoins:
52da3fd565a669b9fb2c5b2e47f55f041dd27928915b4f1155503
0baca6648a5

David sends Sam 20 bitcoins:
db36faee9ba3334271e66131162fdab729e022a0b032f63b7ffc2
54fbd033b18

Hashing these two transactions together will give you this result:

45fcfbd5b60ed42b425c8657dbcdafd16119380baa0897f3f112c
a9c33b23d3e

Just like what happened when you added Block 2 into the blockchain, you would need to have the hashed information from the previous blocks that came before it. Again, to add these transactions as a block, the blockchain network should solve for the nonce.

Now, let's add another block which contains the following transactions:

Sarah sends David 20 bitcoins:
2a2b95ecbeddc12f797557f8352f42ab373a367fb2dc3b0df0b62
6a42a61a9b9

Sam sends David 20 bitcoins:
89db389f104958897ac085d6d3e4e02ec9ae7cce3a97db0a538
606f70e97d2fc

Hashing these transactions together will yield this result:

817345b1519ca6c528060d7c31ecd55e561a9e510d027ade6dc2
a99a3767418e

Again, to add this to the blockchain, you would need to have the hashed value of the previous block and have the network solve for the nonce for this proposed block.

Now that you know all these things, you are ready to mine some bitcoins and verify transactions!

Creating a Blockchain

Now that you know how blocks are created and how they are linked together, you get an idea what makes up a blockchain. As explained in an earlier chapter, blocks that are linked together by their hashes and nonce mined create a blockchain.

Now, how can you create a blockchain for your own private use? Essentially, you would need some programming know-how if you want to create your own blockchain platform. If you are familiar with the programming language Python, then you can create a blockchain and have a genesis block using a few lines of code.

To do that, all you need is to create a code that will allow you to take unique transactions into hashes so you can validate them. Afterwards, you can turn them into a block. For that to happen within Python, you will need to make use of the hash function that will create a unique identifier for your transactions. In turn, the hash function will allow you to link blocks that you can create to each other. Here is a sample of a Python code that can do that:

```
import hashlib, json, sys

def hashMe(msg=""):
    # For convenience, this is a helper function
that wraps our hashing algorithm
    if type(msg)!=str:
        msg = json.dumps(msg,sort_keys=True)  # If
we don't sort keys, we can't guarantee
repeatability!

    if sys.version_info.major == 2:
        return
unicode(hashlib.sha256(msg).hexdigest(),'utf-8')
    else:
        return hashlib.sha256(str(msg).encode('utf-
8')).hexdigest()
```

Image from econmusing.com

Now, you will need to create a function that will allow you to make exchanges possible for two hypothetical people named Bob and Alice. In the following code, you will recognize withdrawals as numbers with a negative sign, while all deposits are denoted as positive numbers.

```
import random
random.seed(0)

def makeTransaction(maxValue=3):
    # This will create valid transactions in the
range of (1,maxValue)
    sign      = int(random.getrandbits(1))*2 - 1
# This will randomly choose -1 or 1
    amount    = random.randint(1,maxValue)
    alicePays = sign * amount
    bobPays   = -1 * alicePays
    # By construction, this will always return
transactions that respect the conservation of
tokens.
    # However, note that we have not done anything
to check whether these overdraft an account
    return {u'Alice':alicePays,u'Bob':bobPays}
```

Image from econmusing.com

Now, you would want to make it easy for you to take a transaction set and then turn them into a block. You can do that by using this line:

```
txnBuffer = [makeTransaction() for i in range(30)]
```

Image from econmusing.com

With this line, you will be able to turn a group of transactions into a block. However, you would want to make sure that your transactions are valid before they get approved to be added into a block.

Let's take the bitcoin blockchain's ability to validate transactions – in this type of blockchain, the input should always be larger than the output, and that transactions should have a key that makes sure that all signatures are valid. In Ethereum, you might recall that smart contracts need to be executed in order for an application to be validated. The sample script will not build a system that is as complicated as the blockchains that you know, but works to create a very basic system that makes use of the token system:

1. When you add the withdrawals and deposits, they should have a value of zero (because tokens cannot be made or destroyed)

2. The user must have enough funds for a withdrawal to be made.

If a transaction violates any of these rules, then the transaction is considered to be invalid.

```
def updateState(txn, state):
    # Inputs: txn, state: dictionaries keyed with account names, holding numeric values for transfer amount (txn) or account balance (state)
    # Returns: Updated state, with additional users added to state if necessary
    # NOTE: This does not not validate the transaction- just updates the state!

    # If the transaction is valid, then update the state
    state = state.copy() # As dictionaries are mutable, let's avoid any confusion by creating a working copy of the data.
    for key in txn:
        if key in state.keys():
            state[key] += txn[key]
        else:
            state[key] = txn[key]
    return state
```

```
def isValidTxn(txn,state):
    # Assume that the transaction is a dictionary
keyed by account names

    # Check that the sum of the deposits and
withdrawals is 0
    if sum(txn.values()) is not 0:
        return False

    # Check that the transaction does not cause an
overdraft
    for key in txn.keys():
        if key in state.keys():
            acctBalance = state[key]
        else:
            acctBalance = 0
        if (acctBalance + txn[key]) < 0:
            return False

    return True
```

Images from econmusing.com

Now that you have an idea on how you can create a script to validate transactions, you can pick up the pace from here, and alter conditions to fit the system that you want to create and then create a block.

To make the blockchain that you are trying to create functional, you need to make sure that you have a way to check the chain's validity. Here is a script that can help you do that:

```
def checkBlockHash(block):
    # Raise an exception if the hash does not match
the block contents
    expectedHash = hashMe( block['contents'] )
    if block['hash']!=expectedHash:
        raise Exception('Hash does not match
contents of block %s'%
                        block['contents']
['blockNumber'])
    return
```

```
def checkBlockValidity(block,parent,state):
    # We want to check the following conditions:
    # - Each of the transactions are valid updates
to the system state
    # - Block hash is valid for the block contents
    # - Block number increments the parent block
number by 1
    # - Accurately references the parent block's
hash
    parentNumber = parent['contents']
['blockNumber']
    parentHash   = parent['hash']
    blockNumber  = block['contents']['blockNumber']

    # Check transaction validity; throw an error if
an invalid transaction was found.
    for txn in block['contents']['txns']:
        if isValidTxn(txn,state):
            state = updateState(txn,state)
        else:
            raise Exception('Invalid transaction in
block %s: %s'%(blockNumber,txn))

    checkBlockHash(block) # Check hash integrity;
raises error if inaccurate
```

```
    if blockNumber!=(parentNumber+1):
        raise Exception('Hash does not match
contents of block %s'%blockNumber)

    if block['contents']['parentHash'] !=
parentHash:
        raise Exception('Parent hash not accurate
at block %s'%blockNumber)

    return state
```

```
def checkChain(chain):
    # Work through the chain from the genesis block
(which gets special treatment),
    #  checking that all transactions are
internally valid,
    #    that the transactions do not cause an
overdraft,
    #    and that the blocks are linked by their
hashes.
    # This returns the state as a dictionary of
accounts and balances,
    #   or returns False if an error was detected


    ## Data input processing: Make sure that our
chain is a list of dicts
    if type(chain)==str:
        try:
            chain = json.loads(chain)
            assert( type(chain)==list)
        except:  # This is a catch-all, admittedly
crude
            return False
    elif type(chain)!=list:
        return False
```

```
    state = {}
    ## Prime the pump by checking the genesis block
    # We want to check the following conditions:
    # - Each of the transactions are valid updates
to the system state
    # - Block hash is valid for the block contents

    for txn in chain[0]['contents']['txns']:
        state = updateState(txn,state)
    checkBlockHash(chain[0])
    parent = chain[0]

    ## Checking subsequent blocks: These
additionally need to check
    #    - the reference to the parent block's hash
    #    - the validity of the block number
    for block in chain[1:]:
        state =
checkBlockValidity(block,parent,state)
        parent = block

    return state
```

Images from econmusing.com

Security of the Blockchain

Now that you have an idea how the blockchain can be built from scratch, you get the idea that being able to validate transactions and know exactly how they occur in the blockchain provides you the transparency that you need. Also, being able to lock transactions in a blockchain allow you to have the peace of mind that everything in the blockchain cannot be changed, which makes it easy for everyone to detect attempts of fraud and keep track of all the changes that are done within the chain.

Take a look at this image:

Inage from blockchain.info

The image above allows you to follow the money, in the most literal sense – you can see here where the bitcoin flows and which bitcoins are left unspent. In a blockchain system, you can trace all transactions from the originator, down to the last node that has an unspent bitcoin.

This data is spread across all computers that participate in the network, and works like a valid document that everybody in the network upholds to be true. If there is an attempt to change a transaction, then the fake data will not match the one that everybody in the blockchain network has, making it very easy for people to know that data manipulation is attempted.

Everybody on the network would simply reject a transaction that makes use of that manipulated data.

The blockchain is built on cooperation – everything that is added to it must be agreed upon by the majority, and at the same time, everybody has all the information they need in order to confirm whether a transaction is valid or not, or when it is confirmed and locked into a block. With decentralization slowly taking place across industries, you may see possibilities that you never thought could happen in a world where traditional fintech giants rule.

Conclusion

Thank you again for purchasing this book, I hope you enjoyed reading it as much as I enjoyed writing it for you!

Finally, if you enjoyed this book I'd like to ask you to leave a review for my book on Amazon, it would be greatly appreciated!

All the best and good luck!

www.ingramcontent.com/pod-product-compliance
Lightning Source LLC
LaVergne TN
LVHW051748050326
832903LV00029B/2784

* 9 7 8 1 7 2 9 5 2 5 5 1 7 *